Conversational Prayer

A constant friendship with Jesus

by
Brother Craig

In Memory of my father
Edward Driscoll - A Man of Prayer

All booklets are published thanks to the
generous support of the members of the
Catholic Truth Society

CATHOLIC TRUTH SOCIETY
PUBLISHERS TO THE HOLY SEE

Contents

'What is a prayer?
It is commonly held to be a conversation.'
Pope John Paul II [1]

Purpose of this book

Throughout this book conversational prayer is written about as a conversation with Jesus. In certain sections I have also explained that you can have a conversation with our Father, the Holy Spirit, Our Lady, Saint Joseph, other Saints or your Guardian Angel. It is my hope and prayer that you will start, if you haven't already, to do conversational prayer.

Although I encourage you to do conversational prayer I am not suggesting you abandon other forms of prayer. Just pray more. I believe forms of prayer are like types of food; we need various ones every day.

Conversational prayer has some very special benefits. It brings us closer to Jesus. It's a friendship form of prayer. It can be done while 'on the go' that is, while working, travelling, shopping and so forth.

Teenagers would benefit greatly from conversational prayer because it is a friendship-type of prayer and no one has a greater capacity for loyal friendship than a teenager. Conversational prayer will bring them into a close or closer friendship with Jesus.

The Value of Prayer

There are, of course, different forms of prayer. We could use various forms of prayer: vocal, mental prayer or meditation, liturgical, charismatic, contemplative, and I like to recommend, conversational prayer. The saddest thing is when people argue one form of prayer against another. One form of prayer may be more special than others. The Liturgy of the Hours, since it is the Prayer of the Church, has priority. The Holy Rosary is very special and has been asked for by Our Lady during many apparitions. The sad thing is to oppose different forms of prayer. I have seen this done. One form of prayer may be more special but it might be very good and indeed God's Holy Will that we pray in another way.

Prayer also can be discussed in terms of degrees. That is, as we pray more and more we ascend to higher stages of prayer. We begin saying vocal prayers, then we do meditation, then more silent and contemplative prayer and perhaps reach stages of infused, that is, mystical prayer. So prayer is a journey. St Teresa of Avila explained it as a journey through the Interior Castle.

By our being faithful to prayer the Holy Spirit will guide us, bringing us to higher stages of prayer. The great teachers of prayer tell us that we prepare ourselves for being brought to these higher stages, usually by striving for greater silence and stillness and greater simplicity in prayer. You may find this happening, in time, with conversational prayer. You will still have a conversation yet use fewer words. This is progress, not a problem. You might also find that you are listening more.

Mary, the Saints and the teachers of prayer have taught us that it is prayer that will lead us to holiness.

What is Conversational Prayer?

Wouldn't you like to be able to talk with Jesus very spontaneously? Wouldn't you like to pray always? You can! By doing conversational prayer!

Conversational prayer is that form of prayer in which we simply talk with or chat with Jesus. We discuss things with Him. In conversational prayer we talk to Jesus naturally and informally about our interests. Perhaps you have tried conversational prayer before and have discovered that the conversation does not last very long. Maybe after a few minutes you cannot think of anything to say. After five sentences or so your mind wanders. I have tried in this booklet to give some helpful hints for prolonging conversational prayer, making it more fruitful and beneficial to your spiritual life.

You could do conversational prayer silently or aloud. Talking aloud during conversational prayer is very enjoyable. You might like to talk to Jesus aloud, perhaps in church alone or on a walk through the woods or when sitting at the seashore.

Before you begin

Perhaps one of the greatest aids to conversational prayer is to realise that, when you talk to Jesus in prayer, you must not restrict your conversation to what you might think is the only appropriate topic: something religious, such as, praise, thanksgiving and petition. This is the key to opening the door to more fruitful and longer conversations with Jesus. You need to add to your conversation what is important to you, your interests and the things you do. If you add these to the conversation with Jesus you will find it enriched and prolonged. Each day you spend time on what is important to you, your interests and certainly on the very things you do. All these will be a 'gold mine' of information for topics of conversation.

We read in *He and I* that Jesus said to Gabrielle Bosis, 'Is it so difficult to talk with me? Everything that interests you, every little detail of your life, tell me about it. I'll listen with such attention and joy. If you only knew. Tell others to talk with me as they would with an intimate friend who knows all the secrets of their hearts.'[2]

How to do Conversational Prayer

Let's consider settling down to do conversational prayer. First try to relax. That's important. Our lives are so busy, we find it hard to slow down. So begin by relaxing. Close your eyes and rest for two or three minutes. Get comfortable. Ever so gently try to be recollected. That means to 'collect' or draw-in the mind and the imagination. Try to be still. Become quite. Rest.

Relax

As mentioned earlier, when you begin your time of conversational prayer—relax. It's good to relax during prayer and to be calm. Sometimes it's good to start our prayer time with some slow deep breathing and to let our bodies go limp in a chair. Some people find it difficult to be relaxed. Relaxing takes effort! If we're tense we have to do certain things to become relaxed. Sometimes we are so tense we think we haven't the patience to do all these things to get relaxed! But we should.

One of the nice things about conversational prayer is that when you are not relaxed, when you are tense and stressed, you can still do conversational prayer. That's right! Just by talking to Jesus about how you're tense. Talk on and on and at the end you'll be more relaxed.

Then gently ask yourself: what's important to me? What are my interests? What have I been doing lately? Each person will have his or her own answer. Here are some possible answers for a mother and housewife: recipes, crafts, reading, knitting, being part of a club, housework and so forth. These are the things that will make the conversation real and make it very enjoyable for her. So the housewife settles down for her time of conversational prayer and says, 'Lord, about the kids and their grades at school,' or, 'Let me tell you about that recipe I just read.' She should discuss all these things with Jesus.

Your favourite subjects

You might have said, after reading the section just before this one, 'Well, it's not religious—about a recipe!' To answer that here's a quotation from *He and I*. Gabrielle writes, 'When Jesus gave me certain good ideas for theater costumes, I said to Him, "You look after these details?" Jesus replied, "In my love for you nothing can be called a detail."' The key to having a very good conversation is to realize that Jesus is interested in everything that is important to us.

If you are interested in literature, poetry, travel or art then these are the subjects to talk to Jesus about. They will help make the conversation enjoyable. If you set all those interests aside and try to talk to Him in a way that does not include them you might find the conversation very short. Why shouldn't you share all your interests with your Best Friend? Hope MacDonald writes, 'I think of prayer as a conversation between friends who love and understand each other.'[3]

An example – GK Chesterton

Here is an example of a conversation I could have with Jesus about one of my favorite people, G.K. Chesterton. 'Jesus, lately I've been reading G.K. Chesterton's life written by Maisie Ward. It's delightful. I've read the book before, although not all of it—you know how I do that! Anyway, it's a great book! The first thing that struck me is that G.K. was a saint and he was very childlike. His holiness is glorious. His childlikeness is so charming.

It's so inspiring to read of G.K.'s great devotion to our Mother, Jesus. His was a childlike devotion. Also, he was our Mother's poet. I love when He says, "One in thy thousand images we salute thee." When he was in Rome, dear Lord, he lost his Miraculous Medal and was quite upset until the bellboy found it. G.K. gave him a large tip.

Jesus, G.K. had such a special devotion to your childhood. He wrote a poem which reads—

"The Christ child stood
at Mary's knee
His hair was like a crown.

All the flowers
looked up at Him
and all the stars
looked down."

Jesus, G.K. was not only childlike but he really loved children. And they loved him. He and his wife, Frances, when travelling by train, tried to choose a compartment filled with children.

Jesus, G.K.'s humility was very inspiring. When he was asked which of his works he thought was the greatest he answered, "I don't consider any of my work in the least great." He seems never to have been offended or to have been angry—even during his public debates. His kindness to those who disagreed with him reminds me of St Thomas Aquinas. Someone said that G.K.'s mind was "strongly co-operative." In his journal we find something he wrote that shows us his great holiness. "I have only one virtue that I know of. I could really forgive seventy times seventy."

Perhaps, dear Jesus, the thing I like about him the most is that he was always cheerful. Actually, the word for him is mirthful!

He said that his life was "indefensibly fortunate and happy." He would sing—not very well Maisie informs us, but she also adds that for him "singing was just making a noise to show he felt happy." His humour was wonderful and famous. He'd joke about himself; about his large size. He taught in one of his books that "Laughter is a leap." I think his humour was related to his humility: he didn't take himself seriously. He once wrote that, "Angels can fly because they take themselves lightly." The beauty of his writing is that, even when he wasn't writing a humourous work, often he was lighthearted or a bit humourous. The same is true of his life—he knew life was serious yet he took it lightly.

G.K. loved the poor so very much. Like Caryll Houselander, he never refused a beggar. At a hotel where G.K. was staying in Warsaw the manager entreated him not to bring every beggar in town around the door.

Jesus, it's so beautiful to read that when G.K. lay dying Father Vincent McNabb picked up G.K.'s pen from a table beside the bed and kissed it. After his death the Holy Father sent a telegram in which he called him a "defender of the Faith." He's so special. Please Jesus, help me to be a little like G.K. Chesterton.'

What have you been doing lately?

Another topic to bring to prayer is what you have been doing lately. If you spent the day at work, shopping, doing errands and so on then in the evening when you settle down to pray talk to Jesus about those experiences.

For example, 'Jesus, I was quite late for work this morning, but I got there. The traffic was terrible. I'll have to leave earlier from now on. About Jane at the office, she has been sick lately. She was out again. Bless her, Jesus, heal her, help her. I know she is not feeling well. Jesus, you take care of her. I'm sorry about that snappy answer I gave the boss. I'll try to be more patient next time. We just get so rushed right before lunch, with so much to do.'

This is a real conversation and real prayer. If, on the way home from work, you went to the supermarket, talk to Jesus about those high prices. Tell Him about the people you've met, and the things you bought.

Talk to Jesus about the things your planning or hope to do soon. 'Jesus, for our vacation this year we would like to visit Mexico.' Discussing your interests and plans is truly conversational prayer.

List your interests

Another help is to make a list of your interests. They need not be in order of importance. The list need not include all of your interests. Here are some of mine:

1. Writing, books about writing and writers' lives.
2. Gardening, growing vegetables and herbs.
3. The Poor, the hungry throughout the world and ways to help them such as our community's Mary's Bread collection.
4. Dorothy Day, the Catholic Worker and pacificism.
5. Reading about people's travels.

6. Saints of early England like St Hilda, St Caedmon the first English poet and St Bede.
7. Health and fitness, jogging and exercise.
8. Children's books. I like to read them to Jesus who lives in the tabernacle in our monastery chapel.
9. Baking Bread.
10. Doodling!

It might sound strange but sometimes—if we are asked—we can't think of our interests. Making a list will help. Pen and paper really help us to think.

Share your plans

Much of conversational prayer can be discussing what you have done, or have been doing lately. There is another way to do it, also. Share your planning with Jesus. Some people only plan a little. They tend to live their days more or less spontaneously. Others are great planners, using date books, notes and agendas.

Share your plans with Jesus. Discuss with Him what you hope to do. Ask Him to guide you; to help you to do His will. Ask His advice. You will enjoy this and make much better plans.

An example – CS Lewis

Here's an example of using some of my plans for conversational prayer.

'Jesus, Gerry is coming tomorrow. We'll be going to Mass at the Benedictines. Then he'll be coming here for lunch. Perhaps I'll see him again on Easter Sunday.

Next week I hope to finish the letters I have to write. Ever since Rick Rotondi introduced me to C.S. Lewis and I read his collected letters to children, I have wanted to write more thoughtful letters. Jesus, C.S. was so charitable. He wrote letter after letter, and not only to children. One letter to a child ends with him apologizing for the letter since he had written it with a terrible headache! Imagine writing a letter with a headache. Jesus, I do hope to read more of C.S. I had, of course, heard of him. Dorothy Day had written that he was her favorite theologian. I had read about him in the biography of J.R.R. Tolkien. But now I hope to read more of his writings. Rick sent me *The Chronicles of Narnia*. I read the first one and most of the second. I didn't realize what they were about until Rick explained them and then I read C.S. Lewis' explanation in some of his letters to children. Dear Jesus, they are about you! They are a story about if you went to another world as its Saviour.'

How long should I pray like this?

How long should you do conversational prayer? As long as you can! This form of prayer need not end when you have to leave the place where you've been praying. Continue the conversation. It doesn't ever have to end. If you really 'collect' your interests you can pray like this for hours.

You should set aside a certain amount of time each day to do conversational prayer. At least a half-hour. It's best to keep to the same time every day just for the sake of discipline.

You might want to have two set times of conversational prayer, perhaps a half-hour in the morning or a half-hour in the evening or a half-hour at midday. Think about it. Talk to Jesus about it and decide what plan is best for you.

Scheduling helps

Having a plan or schedule really helps. If you plan out when you will do conversational prayer and stick to that plan then you will be aided in being faithful to this daily time of prayer. I read a great quotation in a book by Reverend Robert H. Schuller. 'If you fail to plan you plan to fail.' Find the best time for you and schedule your conversational prayer time. Hope Mac Donald wrote: 'To pray well, we must make time to pray. We must set aside a time for prayer each day.' And Archbishop Anthony Bloom taught that, 'if we use crumbs of wasted time to build short moments for recollection and prayer, we may discover that there is quite a lot of it.'

When we schedule our time of conversational prayer we might have to be a bit severe with ourselves in looking at any time wasting we do. The Saints taught that we shouldn't waste time. And they surely didn't. I'm sure Blessed Teresa of Calcutta did not waste a minute! We should carefully examine the last few days or weeks to find out how and when we're wasting time. Perhaps for one person it's reading the newspaper or watching the news. For another it's talking on the phone too long. Time is so precious! It seems that the block of time that is most wasted is from five or six in the evening until bed time. This time is often fritted away. Of course, one might be tired. But that makes the fritting even sadder. When one is tired one needs to rest not frit! So examine your use of time to discover more and more opportunities for conversational prayer.

Our Inner Room

St Catherine of Siena said we should have an inner cell or room into which we can retreat. It's amazing how just imagining ourselves in a quiet, peaceful place can calm and quiet us. By just closing our eyes, by just imagining we are at the ocean—we get calmer and can almost hear the waves.

When we settle down to do conversational prayer we might like to picture ourselves in a room, in the woods or by a lake with Jesus. This might help the conversation.

Writer Hope MacDonald wrote that when she prays she imagines a beautiful room where she and Jesus are together.

Building friendship with Our Lord

Conversational prayer relates very much to friendship with Jesus. The more conversations we have the closer our friendship will become. And the closer our friendship with Jesus the more conversations we will want to have. In the book *He and I* we read that when Gabrielle saw a young married couple on a train, talking tenderly, Jesus said to her, 'If only you talk to Me with the same joy...It would be so simple...So wonderful.' Conversational prayer can lead to a 'Jesus and I' companionship. Some people start calling Jesus by special names such as 'My Friend,' or 'My Beloved.' These names flow from the person's personality and spirituality. You might want to think of one. Some people think of Jesus as their Friend, others their Brother, others their Spouse and so forth. Jesus told Gabrielle, 'Say, "my Jesus." Don't you prefer to be called, "my Gabrielle?"'

This kind of prayer is truly a loving form of prayer, a tete-a-tete or chat between friends. Jesus told Gabrielle, 'Let it be utterly simple and heartwarming, a family chat.'

Talking with Jesus

You might be wondering where you should do conversational prayer. The best place to do conversational prayer is in church in the presence of Jesus. Having a conversation with Jesus who is truly and really present in the tabernacle or monstrance is a wonderful way to pray. If you tried, couldn't you visit Jesus at church each day?

He not only wants to be visited; He waits for these visits. Jesus is loving and lovable. He is sensitive to our love and to our lack of love. We should be thoughtful and visit Him often. We should want to be with Jesus. If it's really impossible there is another way. If you have to do your conversational prayer at home find out where the nearest tabernacle is located. Face that direction and talk to Jesus.

When you pray before the Blessed Sacrament you could kneel or sit or if you prefer, stand. While praying, while having your conversation with Jesus, there is something you should remember, something very important. Jesus in the Blessed Sacrament is the same Jesus of the Gospels. He is the same Person. He is our Best Friend. We need not be rigid or fearful. We should be loving and warm. Talk to Jesus, whether He is in the monstrance or the tabernacle, as you would if you visited Him at the carpenter shop of Nazareth, friend to Friend.

Thanksgiving after Holy Communion

The best time to do conversational prayer is after Holy Communion. Try to spend a half-hour after Mass talking to Jesus. It will transform your spiritual life! Here are some examples.

'Jesus, I have you. Thank you! It's so wonderful, to receive you. You're in my heart. When I receive you I feel so recollected. So calm. It's nothing I can do myself. It reminds me of what the English poet, Edith Sitwell's secretary said of her. "That the calmness she had after Holy Communion was not integral to her." That's true for me. The recollection, the calmness, the pulling inward they are not of me, nor of prayer. They are from you. From you within me. Thank you for the sunshine coming into the chapel. Please, Jesus, bless Mrs. Paulin; she is sick today. Please help Brian's wife, Alice, and the baby she carries. Alice is in the hospital, quite sick, Mrs. Paulin called for prayers. Please heal her and watch over the baby. I haven't seen Brian in two years.' (The baby was born in perfect health).

'Jesus, I'm really excited. This morning I spoke with Brother Ambrose, one of the Benedictines. We had a marvellous conversation about Ray who is a friend of our friend, Mark Sebanc and his family. Ray visited their home in Canada way out in the country. They home-school their five children. Brother is very interested in the Amish. Brother told me about Erik Brende and his wife who live simply on a farm next to an Amish community in Kentucky, I told Brother about visiting the Catholic Worker in New York and how impressed I was with them! We talked about farming communities and the group at New Hope, Kentucky. It was a wonderful conversation—and so is this one!

Jesus, here I am. We're together. Thank you, for this Holy Communion! Thank you for being with me. You are so nice, so kind and so special. No wonder I love you!

Well, let's see. This morning I was thinking about the Enid Dinis book. I'd like to collect some of her stories and perhaps get them published. I especially would like—though it's a long novel—to get the *Shepherd of Weeping Wold* reprinted. Guide me; help me make all the right decisions about this.

By the way, I haven't heard from the editor in England about the sample I sent for the column there. Nor have I heard about the suggestion for another column for the Catholic Twin Circle. Jesus, I think I need a secretary!

I feel a little tired. Help me, dear Love, to organize my life better, especially the writing. I offer receiving you this morning for the intention of being more organised.'

Talking with the Holy Spirit, the Sanctifier

We should pray often to the Holy Spirit. We should talk to him. Since the Holy Spirit is the Sanctifier, the One who makes us holy, we should talk to him about holiness, about our spiritual life. We must be careful to remember the Holy Spirit. It is also perhaps good to take part in Charismatic prayer meetings and to attend seminars toward receiving the Baptism of the Holy Spirit.

The Holy Spirit dwells within us. He is our Friend, our Companion. We should ask the Holy Spirit to bring ever more alive His Gifts that are within us. Let us talk with the Holy Spirit about His wondrous Gifts: Filial Fear, Fortitude, Piety, Counsel, Knowledge, Understanding and

Wisdom. And speak of His marvelous Fruits: Charity, Joy, Peace, Patience, Goodness, Benignity, Longanimity, Mildness, Faith, Modesty, Contentment and Chastity. We should talk about our Confirmation with the Holy Spirit. It is such a precious grace.

The Holy Spirit as the Sanctifier makes us holy by forming us, making us like Jesus, for the glory of the Father. This wonderful doctrine was taught by Archbishop Luis M. Martinez (d. 1956) who was the Archbishop of Mexico City. The rest of the quotations in this section are from his book *The Sanctifier*. This holy Archbishop was the spiritual director of two great Mexican mystics. They were Conception Cabrera Armida, also called Conchita (d. 1938) and Mother Auxilia (d. 1974) the foundress of the Oblates of the Blessed Sacrament.

In *The Sanctifier* the Archbishop writes that the Holy Spirit is our teacher. 'He teaches us by pouring Himself into us gently and penetratingly. His teaching is as a divine caress of love. He teaches us as mothers teach their children, with kisses of love, with an indefinable outpouring of tenderness. We learn from Him as we would perceive the fragrance of a perfume, as we savor the sweetness of a fruit, or enjoy the caress of a breeze that enfolds us.' We must pay attention to this teaching, be attentive and have a loving relationship with the Holy Spirit. 'Our chief concern and duty toward the Divine

Guest is to try to be with Him. But it is even better to treat Him affectionately, to be with Him while He is under our roof, to look at Him, to speak to Him and listen to Him, to give Him signs of friendship and love.'

We need to be docile to the gentle inspirations of the Holy Spirit. 'In order to attain this holy docility to the motions of the Spirit, the soul must be so silent and recollected so that it can hear His voice.'[3a]

The Holy Spirit will form us into 'another' Jesus. He will mold us so that we can be Jesus for others. Becoming like Jesus is the essence of sanctity. 'Fully to glorify the Father it is necessary to be transformed into Jesus; because the glorification of the Father is his work.'

Archbishop Martinez explains that in forming us and making us like Jesus for the glory of the Father, the Holy Spirit forms us according to a particular aspect of the life of Jesus. That aspect is our mission. It is our vocation. The sooner we learn what this is, the better. To learn this pray to the Holy Spirit, talk to Him and listen.

Talking with Our Lady and the Saints

It is wonderful to talk with our Mother. Truly mothers love to have their children with them. Each day spend some time talking with Our Blessed Mother. You'll love it!

Chat with your Mother—for Our Lady truly is your Mother. I think a good way to talk with Our Lady is to sit in the kitchen, say, around ten or eleven in the morning and have a cup of coffee or tea and have a conversation with Mum. Be together. Become closer. She loves you so. Talk with Mother every day. Jesus told Gabrielle, 'When you talk to my Mother, be one with me as I poured out my Heart to her on the earth.'

What should you talk to your Mother about? Well, you can talk about your interests, the things you do or your work. Your Mother wants to hear all about these things. Tell Mum about your sorrows, your sufferings. She truly understands for she suffered so much when her Son, Jesus, was made to suffer. Tell Mum about your joys, especially when you get good news. Run and tell your Mother. Let her be the first to know. Spend a set time each day talking together. Then chat with your Mother throughout the day. Share your day with her. You'll enjoy it so much. So will Mum.

In talking to Our Lady about my interests I like to talk about the Poor in the world, the hungry, the starving. Our community started a special collection called Mary's Bread. I could spend an afternoon talking to Mum about the hungry and about this apostolate. I could talk about the motto for this apostolate, 'He has filled the hungry with good things' from her Magnificat. And I could share with Our Blessed Mother a quote I recently discovered. The French Dominican Father Thomas Phillipe, O.P., wrote, 'Mary is the compassionate Mother; the poor, the little ones, the disinherited are the object of her predilection. She goes first to them, for their need is greater.'

Or since I love the root meaning of words I could talk to Our Lady about how the word 'lady' comes from the Old English 'hlaefdge' with 'hlaef' meaning loaf and 'dige' akin to the word 'daege' meaning kneader of bread. 'So lady means kneader of a loaf,' I could tell my Mother.

Spend some time talking with Mother each day about your interests. Talk to Our Lady about your hopes, plans, dreams and fears. These conversations will help you to grow in a trusting relationship with Our Blessed Mother.

Saint Joseph

You really should talk to St Joseph. He's wonderful. He's so helpful. It's especially helpful to talk to him about working, building, employment and financial matters. St Joseph is truly a good provider and he understands problems of economy and employment very well. Dorothy Day, who always prayed to Saint Joseph for the financial needs of the Catholic Worker, called him 'Saint Joseph, the Householder.'

He is the protector of the Church and will be pleased when we ask his intercession for the Church. St Joseph is also called the terror of demons in his litany and we should tell him how much we want his help in rejecting the devil.

During our conversation we could think of Saint Joseph planing a piece of wood. Or listening as Jesus offers to sweep up. I think the greatest occupation (priesthood being a vocation) is to be a carpenter. Spend time, each day, talking with Saint Joseph the Carpenter.

The Saints

It's good to have a conversation with one of the Saints. It's enjoyable to have a conversation with a Saint about his or her special interest. Try to learn what these are. Reading the lives of the Saints will give you much to talk about during your conversation. Here are some special interests of certain Saints:

St John Bosco—youth in need

St Francis Xavier—poor immigrants.

St Gemma—suffering to help save souls.

St Jeanne Jugan—poor abandoned elderly.

St Margaret Mary—devotion to the Sacred Heart
of Jesus.
St Michael—protection from the devil.
St Elizabeth Ann Seton—the education of children.
St Vincent de Paul—the poor and orphans.
St Peter Julian Eymard—adoration of the
Blessed Sacrament.

Or if you read the life of a particular Saint then you'll
have lots to talk about with that Saint. Reading the lives of
the Saints is a great inspiration and you'll find that certain
Saints will become your special friends. You'll feel as if
you've met them. How I have enjoyed reading the lives of
various Saints, such as St Francis, St Benedict, St
Madeline Sophie Barat, St Dominic, St John of the Cross,
St Teresa of Avila, the Cure of Ars, St Gemma, St
Margaret Mary, St Vincent de Paul, St Benedict Joseph
Labre and so many more! Many people have a special
friendship and not only a special devotion with St Thérèse
of Lisieux. Others have a special closeness to St Anthony
or St Jude. Sometimes one can't even explain why. Love is
like that. People just have their favorite Saints.

Talking about problems and sufferings

Your conversations with Jesus should be about what is
important to you. It could be about problems. Certainly
if you have a problem, talk to Jesus, Our Lady or the

Saints about it. But don't restrict the conversation to problems. Don't just talk to your Heavenly Friends when you have a problem.

When you are suffering you need to pray. When you are suffering you should talk to Jesus. He understands. Soren Kierkegaard, the saintly Danish philosopher and religious writer, tells us that the whole life of Jesus was one of suffering. When you are in pain, be it physical, mental or spiritual you need to turn to Jesus, to talk to Him. Tell Him all about what you are going through. Ask for the grace of acceptance. Ask for a healing. Ask Him to be with you; to hold you close.

Suffering saves souls. It can make us a holy, gentle saint. But we can't do it alone. We need Jesus. We need to unite our sufferings with the sufferings of Jesus and His Mother. We need to talk to Him. Like the beautiful African-American spiritual song says, 'Nobody know the troubles I got. Nobody knows, but Jesus.'

Sometimes when we are in pain we cannot pray in the usual sense. Perhaps we can talk. Perhaps we are talking to friends and relatives. Let us talk to Jesus, also. Tell Him your needs and hopes. He understands.

Your Guardian Angel

God has given us an Angel to guard us and to guide us. We call this Angel our Guardian Angel and rightly so. Yet, this Angel is also our 'Guidian' Angel with a mission to guide and inspire us. Our Angel gives us many good ideas, which we might think are our own! We should listen to our angel, ask for help and pray to our Angel. We should be grateful to our Angel. And, of course, we should talk to our Angel.

Each day spend some time chatting with your Angel. Be sure to express gratitude for such wonderful care! Talk to your Angel about your needs and your plans after all you'll be doing everything together. So talk about it together!

Praying Always and Everywhere

One reason conversational prayer is so handy is that it can be prayed anywhere—at home, at work, in school, walking or jogging. At home you might like to try sitting in a comfortable chair or on a couch. Since this is a relaxed form of prayer, a relaxed position might be best.

Sometimes you might seek a special place for conversational prayer, perhaps the seashore on a cool Autumn day. Wearing a sweater, sitting on a rock, you could pray conversationally for hours as you watch the seagulls. Or perhaps a walk in the woods is what you'd like. You might find that you can do conversational prayer very well riding in a car on a long trip. I think that the greatest treat is to pray while riding on a train gazing out the window looking at the countryside. C.S. Lewis loved to pray on a train.

When you exercise or jog or do your brisk walking you could do conversational prayer. Or while you eat. That's right. Have lunch or supper with Jesus. Be together. Talk together. Then chat with Jesus while doing the dishes. If you're in the house alone these conversations could be aloud.

Narrational prayer

Conversational prayer enables us to 'pray always.'
Perhaps you've tried to pray always and found it difficult.
But with conversational prayer it's possible, especially
with a version I call 'narrational prayer.' This is when we
simply narrate what we are doing. It's very easy. Ignore
the thought that says, 'But Jesus already knows what I'm
doing.' He wants to hear about what you are doing—in
your own words. By narrating what you're doing you'll
be praying for hours! Rather than try to explain it further
here's an example of what could be narrational prayer for
one of the Brothers here at our monastery.

'Jesus, I have to go to the country store here in town.
Please come with me. Accompany me. Please don't let
me forget Your presence. We need some bread. Then I
have to go to the Post Office. Oh! I nearly forgot the car
keys...Jesus, there's Mrs. Flynn. Bless her Lord. It must
be difficult living all alone now that her husband died.
Jesus, let's visit her this afternoon...Now, we're at the
store. Please bless all the people I see...Jesus, I'll buy this
bread, I think the Brothers will like it...my Friend, the
clerk seemed very tired today, bless her, help her...Now,
Jesus, let's go to the Post Office and pick up the mail and
see how many bills we've received! Yes, I know St Joseph
is in charge of that!... Oh, here's a letter from Rosalie.
She's so special. Bless her apostolate, dear Jesus. She

loves our Mother so much and works so hard promoting the messages from her apparitions...Well, Jesus, we're home. Thank you for going with me; Stay with me all day. I'll keep you informed about all I'm doing! I don't want to do anything without you. I love you.'

When with others

Could you continue talking to Jesus when you are having a conversation with others? Yes, you can! It's great! When you're talking to other people your part of the conversational prayer doesn't continue. But when they are talking, you can tell Jesus what they are saying. Ask Him to bless them, heal them and help them. This is a great way to do intercessory prayer. You don't have to worry about remembering (or forgetting!) to pray for the person later. Pray right then and there. Talk to Jesus when you are grocery shopping or walking through a store or a parking lot or doing errands or anywhere. Once Jesus told Gabrielle that she was the only one in a train station praying. So wherever you go remember the presence of Jesus and talk to Him constantly. You'll both love it.

Another good thing to do is to pray for the people you see. As you walk or ride down a street you could talk to Jesus about the people you pass. Some people who do this think of it as shooting love at these people. Sometimes the people they were praying for have all of a sudden smiled at them!

Be yourself

It's really important during conversational prayer to be yourself. Be you! Talk to Jesus as you, as the 'who you really are.' Yes, Jesus wants you to be a Saint—but He wants you to be Saint You. So often, after reading a life of a Saint, we strive to be holy just like that Saint. Sometimes this attitude misleads us. For we have our own mission and vocation. In reading the lives of the Saints we should allow their inspiration to help us fulfill God's will for us. This reading should also help us to fulfill our duties. And when you have a conversation with Jesus be sincerely you!

Listening

Of course, a conversation involves listening. During our time of conversational prayer there should be periods of silence, too. After talking to Jesus for a while we should listen. Ask Jesus what He has to say to you and then listen. Do not try to hear, just listen. What is the difference? When we try to hear, like when the radio is on too low, we strain, we concentrate, we make an effort to hear. But when we just listen we do not try so hard. We just listen. When we listen to the waves at the seashore, perhaps breaking on the rocks, we just listen. We listen to the waves, the seagulls, the wind. Noise of nearby traffic we do not hear. Somehow we've tuned it out. We are listening but without strain. That's how we should listen during conversational prayer.

Your spiritual life

Another subject for conversational prayer is your spiritual life. By having a conversation with Jesus about your spiritual life you can grow in holiness. Talk with Jesus about those wonderful virtues, such as humility, meekness, simplicity, being little, being kind and about being very, very gentle and compassionate. Talk with Jesus about how much you trust Him and how, each day, you want to grow in confidence. Let Jesus guide your spiritual life. Let Him mold you. Open your heart to Jesus during these conversations.

Ask Jesus to lead you to the heights of holiness by way of childlike trust and confidence. Too many people try to be holy by way of scruples and fear. By frequent loving conversations with Jesus you'll be guided away from avenues of doubt and worry and you'll be carried in the arms of Jesus to holiness and Heaven.

Mementos

Things or objects can be used to aid us during conversational prayer. Especially things that are truly mementos, really bring back pleasant memories. It might be a letter or a picture from an enjoyable holiday. You could take this reminder or memento in your hand and talk to Jesus about the memories it brings. Learn to reminisce with Jesus. Older people might find this especially pleasant as they walk down memory lane with Jesus. You could use a favorite painting or print. Maybe a special figurine, perhaps a Hummel or something like that. After all, it's something you cherish and surely you are thankful to God for it. Take it in your hands or just look at it and talk to Jesus about it.

Music

You might find that listening to music helps you with your conversational prayer. Keep the music a little low so that it's background music. I would like Chamber Music.

I have other favorites, too. Sue Ann Pinner and the Santa Barbara Regional Choir produced a marvelous Ave Maria CD[4]. One side has ten versions of the Ave Maria and the other has various Marian Hymns. It is like being in Heaven. Other types of music I enjoy are those of flute music or the harp. I have a tape of several piano solos that makes me feel very calm. The music you choose could be listened to and discussed with Jesus.

Films

Though good films are hard to find, when one does find a really enjoyable one it can help conversational prayer in two ways. It can be a subject of conversation during the film and after. When I watch a good film I talk to Jesus and Mary as I watch it. Having watched it, now, it can be a topic of conversation.

When you are watching a video or enjoying a really good film talk to Jesus about it. After it's over, rather than let it be a distraction to prayer, have it be a help to prayer.

Letters

Letters and letter writing can be a very real part of conversational prayer. If you write letters and receive them and enjoy doing so then you could talk about them with Jesus. Letters that are truly part of a real correspondence between friends can really give you things to talk about during conversational prayer. Newsy letters with much information will give you lots to talk about. You can talk about both the letters you receive and the ones you write. You could read them to Jesus. You could write Jesus a letter! That would be a written conversation.

Those who keep a journal might find it helpful to use the journal during conversational prayer for ideas. I only recently started keeping a journal. I found it took a while to get the 'swing' of journal-writing. But I'm enjoying it. Read to Jesus from your journal or talk about it. Or write in the journal by writing to Jesus.

The idea is to bring all your interests to Jesus and bring Jesus to all your interests.

Special Prayers and Meditation

Devotions

Special prayers, such as the Stations of Cross and the Holy Rosary can benefit from the practice of conversational prayer. As you are praying at each Station you could talk to Jesus and Our Sorrowful Mother offering them love, compassion and reparation. During the praying of the Holy Rosary alone you could stop now and then and talk to Jesus and Mary about the Mystery. Or you could say something to Our Lord and Our Lady— when praying the Rosary with others—during the time when you are silent.

One can even say some things conversationally during liturgical prayer. Formal prayers, like novenas, can be done conversationally. I did a novena to Don Bosco before his feast (January 31) that was really just a little conversation with him each day. Do a conversational novena to your favorite Saint. You'll really enjoy it.

Meditation

If you do meditation you could add a bit more conversation to it. When I was a student in Rome my spiritual director taught me a way of meditation called C.A.R. Here's how it's done.

Consideration—of, perhaps, a Gospel text.
Application—of the consideration to one's own life.
Resolution—make a resolution based on the
consideration and the application.

Meditation is a very important form of prayer. It is
really the form that leads to the higher stages of prayer,
such as contemplation. It is the doorway from vocal
prayer to deeper and more recollected forms of prayer. It
is truly a life-changing form of prayer for it leads us to
make well-considered and well-motivated resolutions.

How does conversation enter into meditation? After
thinking about the subject of the meditation, perhaps the
Visitation, you could speak to Jesus or Mary about this
very special event, discuss how it applies to your life and
make a resolution, perhaps to visit someone in need more
often. Conversation should be the heart of meditation.

You could, also, use a meditation from a book of
meditations as the subject for your conversation.

The Sacred Passion

We should meditate upon the Passion of Jesus. St
Augustine wrote that one tear shed over the Sacred
Passion of Jesus is better than fasting on bread and water
for a year. Meditating or thinking about the sufferings of
Our Lord and the sorrows of Our Blessed Mother can be
done in a conversational way. We can talk to Jesus and

Mary about the sorrows they suffered in Jerusalem. Books telling about the Passion are a help.

Petitions

Praying for others is certainly very important and it can be done conversationally. You can pray for your loved ones and your friends during conversational prayer. You can have a very beautiful time of prayer by talking to Jesus about those in need. You can mention them by name, tell about their problems or needs and ask for blessings, graces and healings. This will benefit these people because you are praying and it will bring you closer to them. You could even have a special time during your daily period of conversational prayer to make these intercessions; perhaps at the very beginning or at the end.

Jesus said to Gabrielle, 'From the moment you wake up, intercede for others. Claim sinners from Me. You cannot know the joy you would give me. I died for them. It wasn't illness that made me die. I was struck down in the fullness of life. If you don't help me today I won't be able to save this or that one and you know I love them. Then save them as though you were saving me.'

One good thing to do when we pray for someone with a need is also to pray for everyone who has that need. If I pray for my Aunt Agatha who is sick I should add to my prayer all those who are sick. This widens our love and concern.

It's nice to pray for people by name. When people ask me to pray for someone saying, 'Would you pray for my daughter who is sick?'—I ask for her name. It helps me to remember to pray for that person. Also, praying for someone by name seems more natural for conversational prayer.

The Holy Souls

We can talk about, that is, pray for the Holy Souls in Purgatory by conversational prayer. We can ask Jesus to help them, to bring them to Heaven. If we know them personally we can talk about the good times we had together. We can also pray to the Holy Souls. Though they are not able to pray for themselves, they can pray for us. We can talk to our loved ones who have 'gone ahead.' We can ask Our Lady to help them. We can talk about our deceased loved ones and pray for them by name.

Reading with Jesus

Jesus told Gabrielle, 'When you read, don't be with the author of the book. Be with me.' It is wonderful to read a book with or to Jesus. You can read books to Jesus at a nearby church. Or you can do this at home. How do you read a book with or to Jesus? First, pick a book, perhaps a book of spiritual reading. Perhaps not. Then settle down in a comfortable chair if you are at home. Maybe with a cup of coffee! Begin by telling Jesus that you want to remember His presence as you read the book. Stop every now-and-then and chat with Jesus about the book. Tell Him what you think of it. Talk about special passages. Even re-read them to Him. Then read a little more and talk again. This is a little difficult to describe but if you try it you will really enjoy it. I especially love to read poetry with Jesus or children's stories. Surely, you have your own favorites.

Even without a book in my hand, without reading, I enjoy talking to Jesus about some of my favorite books, or stories or authors. During conversational prayer I could tell Him about how I recently read *Little Men* by Louisa May Alcott and talk about what an extraordinary work that is, not only a delightful story but a fine lesson about education based on Louisa's father, Broxson Alcott's, principles. That would lead me to talk about the time I visited the Alcott's house—'Orchard House.' I would mention that Louisa preferred to call the house 'Apple Slump.' That would remind me to talk about how much I like apples, especially Cortlands and of the time I bought a bushel at an orchard in New Salem. Or more about my visit to Concord, Massachusetts; to Emerson's house, the Thoreau museum and to Nathaniel Hawthorne's house which is where the Alcotts also had once lived. I could then go on for an hour especially if I had *Little Men* in my hands and read bits from it. All this would remind me of Rose Hawthorne, who, after becoming a Catholic, founded an order of Dominican Sisters who care for cancer patients. I would also think of Margaret Sidney (Mrs. Lothrop) who lived in Hawthorne's house after buying it from Rose. She wrote the *Little Pepper* children's books and she and her husband published several children's magazines.

The point I am trying to make is not that all this taken from Concord will necessarily be your conversation. But another book could start you off!

Sacred Scripture

Reading the Word of God will surely help our prayer life. We should spend time every day reading the Holy Bible. As we read we'll grow in our love and appreciation of Sacred Scripture. We should read it humbly and with reverence. Perhaps we won't understand everything. No matter. It will transform our souls. We should read the Holy Bible every day. Perhaps we need a daily plan or a system.

The Church must be the one to interpret Sacred Scripture for us. We must remember that for many years, until about the year 50 A.D. the Church existed before the first of the New Testament was written. Before the New Testament was given to us the Church decided what writings would be included in it, that is, which were inspired by the Holy Spirit. The Church has given us the Word of God. As Catholics we look to the Church to interpret the meaning of Sacred Scripture. Yet we must not leave it to the Church to read it for us! We must read the Bible. Many other Christians put us to shame when it comes to Bible reading—may we be shamed into changing! Yes, some Catholics do read God's Word as piously as Baptists, but many do not.

Although when we read the Holy Bible we leave interpretation to the Church we may and should let God's Word speak to us. 'To our condition' as the Quakers say. A passage strikes us, a phrase inspires us, a verse or chapter enlightens, heals, helps, or converts us. Each day we should nourish ourselves on Sacred Scripture. Then, having spent time reading the Bible let's talk to Jesus about it. Let's bring our Bibles (well worn, I hope) to our place of conversational prayer and discuss certain passages with Jesus.

Each of us reads the Bible differently. Each of us has an angle on our reading. During conversational prayer you can talk with Jesus about the passages that touch you. He might explain them. Is He not The Teacher? So together you'll talk—You, the disciple, the pupil; He, the Master or Teacher. You'll have a wonderful conversation! Perhaps read a passage to Jesus. You can talk about certain passages—'Turn the other cheek'—'Do good to those who persecute you'—'If a man takes your coat give him your cloak as well.' And ask lots of questions like—'What was a coat and what was a cloak in your day Jesus?' What better way to spend an afternoon?

Humour

It might seem surprising to have a section on humour in a book about prayer. But I believe that a sense of humour is not only necessary to be sane and healthy but it helps us to be holy. And it helps us to pray. Humour can help us to throw off anger and depression. It can help us forgive people. By adding humour to tense situations we can release stress and tension.

Shouldn't you sometimes be humourous when you talk to Jesus? Aren't you sometimes funny when you talk to your other friends? When you hear a funny story or when something strikes you as funny, share it with Jesus, make it part of your conversation.

The holy Mexican mystic, Conchita, who founded several religious communities and apostolates, had a notebook of her favorite jokes! St Teresa of Avila, St John Bosco, St Thomas More were known for their humour. The funniest Saint of all seems to have been St Philip Neri who, when at the Vatican, would tug on the beards of the Swiss Guards. Perhaps that's why they no longer have beards!

The devil hates laughter. We, on the contrary, should love it. St Teresa of Avila prayed asking to be preserved from meeting sullen, saintly people. St Maximillian Kolbe would laugh with his fellow religious until he cried. St Thérèse of Lisieux would do impersonations for the other nuns during their time of recreation. When she was absent the sisters said there would be no fun that day.

So let's be holy and happy. Jansenism is the heresy that wants us to be sad, serious and fearful. Scruples are the devil's trick to turn us inward and to take all joy from our lives. Rather, let's frolic with the freedom of the Children of God. Let's dance to cheerful tunes played by angels and let's laugh. Yes, life is serious and there are many problems to bear. That's why we need to laugh! A little sign a friend has reads: 'Don't take life too seriously. It's only a temporary situation.' So let's be holy, humble, happy and humourous. Let's remember the words of Hilaire Belloc,

'Wherever a Catholic sun does shine
there's always laughter and good red wine.'

We need to laugh. It helps us to take life less seriously, to be less tense and more relaxed. Humour helps. It 'lifts up our hearts' as we pray at Mass. So let's be humourous as we do conversational prayer and make Jesus laugh!

As a little child

A great help to conversational prayer is to be childlike. This, of course, is necessary to obey Jesus who said we would not enter the Kingdom of Heaven—unless we become as a little child. Being childlike greatly helps conversational prayer. First, by having a childlike interest in many things, a real wonder about many wonderful things, we will have a lot to talk about! Added to this, a childlike simplicity, honesty and openness will help us to share our interests with Jesus. As the writer and great teacher of prayer, Rosalind Rinker wrote, 'Pray to Jesus from the child in your heart'.

Gentle compassion

Some things just put us in a prayerful mood. Some activities just seem to quiet or calm us. Others make us nervous. Some things make us peaceful. Anne Morrow Lindbergh wrote: 'Arranging a bowl of flowers in the morning can give a sense of quiet in a crowded day—like writing a poem or saying a prayer'. Just as being calm and relaxed helps us to pray I think that to be gentle, to be kind, to have great compassion helps us to pray. It helps us to have a prayerful attitude.

When we are kind and loving we feel good about others and about ourselves. Of course, when we are angry or resentful or bitter we, at least, don't feel very prayerful. So another reason for being gentle and compassionate is to help us to pray well. Let us meditate on the Gospel passages that teach kindness, being gentle, compassion, forgiveness and returning good for evil.

Let us be kind and gentle to all, to people and to animals or, as the Buddhists say, to all sentient or feeling beings. This will help us to pray.

Lessons on Prayer

Distractions

We must not worry about distractions during prayer. Jesus told Gabrielle, 'If you have the intention of loving me when you pray, I'll accept your prayer even when you are distracted.'

Conversational prayer in itself is very helpful regarding distractions. Sometimes those very distractions can be made part of the conversation. Let's say you are a writer and you just had an article accepted by a Catholic magazine. You're all excited and it's on your mind all day long and when it's your prayer time you settle down to pray and you keep thinking about the article. You're trying to say things to Jesus while fighting the distractions about the article. Don't do it! Jesus wants to hear about the article, too. Of course, He knows about it but He wants you to tell Him about it. You could say, 'Jesus, thank you that the article was accepted. I'm all excited; I can't wait to see it in print. I'll send Aunt Rose a copy.' Then you go on for an hour with what would have been a distraction!

Noise

Surely noise can be a problem when you are trying to pray. One help regarding noise is to do what St Thérèse did. One Sister in the chapel made noises with her teeth. It really bothered St Thérèse who had sensitive hearing. It stopped bothering her when she accepted the noise and offered the hearing of it to God as a sacrifice.

It's mainly our resistance to disturbance that disturbs us. So relax. Accept it. Offer the noise as a sacrifice. However, noise is really less of a problem for conversational prayer for you can talk about the noise as part of your conversation!

Recollected or not

Recollection is very important for prayer. Before starting our time of conversational prayer we should try to quiet our minds. However, one of the great benefits of conversational prayer is that even when we cannot pray recollectedly, meaning that our minds are racing, we're a nervous wreck and we've had the most hectic day since kindergarden, we can still pray! Perhaps I should have sub-titled this 'A Way to Pray for New York Cab Drivers.' When we are very unrecollected, when the whole world is racing around us and we're racing also—only in the opposite direction—then is the time for conversational prayer. Then we should talk like mad! Talk, talk, talk! Tell Jesus all about it. Explain, repeat, re-explain and even exaggerate. Laugh, cry, sigh and talk it over and talk it out!

I think this is one of the greatest benefits of conversational prayer. Talkative people will agree! When your mind is racing like a speeding train don't try to stop it. That will cause a crash! Just start talking to your Best Friend. He's the greatest listener. He cares so much. So start with, 'Wait till You hear this' and continue through till, 'That's not the half of it!' You'll have a wonderful conversation.

Dryness

Any form of prayer can be difficult. We can experience dryness. We can feel like a stone. We are going through a desert. We should keep praying as best we can. We should not shorten our prayer time. We must keep at it without strain or tension. We might just say, 'Here I am, Jesus. I feel like a stone. But I love you and want to be with you.'

Of course, when you are doing conversational prayer one of the things you can talk about is prayer. You can discuss things you've read about prayer, or talk about how you are doing, how you are praying and so forth.

St Teresa of Avila

A very helpful book is *The Way of Perfection* by St Teresa of Avila. It's a book not only about prayer but a book that inspires a friendship-relationship with Jesus. It is St Teresa who defines prayer as a conversation! She wrote that 'prayer is a conversation with God whom we know loves us.' Truly, *The Way of Perfection* is a delightful book. You will be learning from a master. In the prologue to the book St Teresa states: 'I shall speak of nothing of which I have not experience either in my own life or in observation of others or which the Lord had not taught me in prayer.'[5] Also, reading St Teresa's autobiography known as the *Life* and her masterpiece *The Interior Castle* are wonderful experiences. Reading a biography of St Teresa is a delightful meeting with a most loving, humorous, and common sense friend. Those who are friends with 'La Madre' consider her a great companion to have—she teaches them to pray, to play the castanets and to let 'nothing disturb them.' Saint Teresa has been my friend for some years now, ever since I bought her autobiography when I was at university. She'll help you to do conversational prayer for she's the doctor of the Church whom we call 'The Doctor of Prayer.'

Brother Lawrence and the presence of God

Two great teachers of prayer were Brother Lawrence and Frank Lauback. Brother Lawrence of the Resurrection was a holy Carmelite Brother who was born in 1614 and died in Paris in 1691. As a Carmelite he spent most of his life working in the kitchen. St Teresa of Avila wrote that the 'Lord walks among the pots and pans.' Brother Lawrence's spirituality was centered on the Presence of God. That is, being aware of God's Presence. He wrote several letters regarding this. In time, after his death, they were published as a small book along with remembered conversations and some maxims he wrote. They have been cherished by many Christians.

One Christian missionary who really liked Brother Lawrence's book was a man named Frank Laubac. He also developed a widely used system of teaching people to read, for which there was a thirty-cent U.S. stamp dedicated to him. Frank not only appreciated Brother Lawrence's book but wrote a booklet to help implement the good Brother's teaching. It's called *A Game With Minutes*.[6]

The title refers to the 'game' we should play wherein we try to recall or be aware of God's Presence during as many minutes as possible. I was given this book by my friend, Dorothy, a Benedictine Oblate. She gave it to me because I had told her that I was not able to implement what I read in Brother Lawrence's book. I found Frank Lauback's book very helpful. There are a couple of helpful suggestions from this book I wish to share as a help to conversational prayer. Have a picture of Jesus before you when you pray. St Teresa of Avila had also suggested this. Then during conversational prayer you can talk toward the picture as you talk to Jesus. Also, when out walking, to remind you to talk to Jesus, walk to one side (say, of the sidewalk) and imagine Jesus walking beside you.

I recently discovered a beautiful story, an application of this imagining of Jesus beside oneself, in a book by

Reverend Norman Vincent Peale. He quoted the story from Reverend Leslie Weatherhead, of an old Scotsman who was very ill. He was visited by his minister. The old man explained the reason for the empty chair near his bed. Years before he found his mind wandered when he prayed. A minister advised him, 'Do not think you must kneel to pray. Just sit down and put a chair opposite and imagine that Jesus is in it and talk to Him as you would to a long time friend.' The man confided, 'I've been doing it ever since and it works.' Some time later the old man died. His daughter told the minister that he had died alone and was found, she couldn't understand why, with his hand resting on a chair near his bed. The minister understood.

St Thérèse of Lisieux

Since trust and confidence are such a help to conversational prayer I recommend you read *The Story of a Soul* by St Thérèse of Lisieux, Doctor of the Church. This book will really set you on the way of trust and confidence, the way of spiritual childhood. The book is truly magnificent. St Thérèse was a writer of genius. She has given us not only a great spiritual book but a great literary work as well. However, some people find that it is only after they read it a second time does the message really dawn on them. There must be a lesson in that! Reading the letters of St Thérèse also is rewarding and inspiring.[7]

Sister Mary of the Holy Trinity

A good book to read as you make conversational prayer part of your life is the *Spiritual Legacy of Sister Mary of the Holy Trinity*. The book contains the words of Jesus to Sister Mary of the Holy Trinity, a Swiss Poor Clare Nun who lived at the Poor Clare monastery in Jerusalem and died in 1942. I visited Sister's monastery in Jerusalem and prayed at her grave in their cemetery. The words spoken by Jesus to this good Sister inspire great trust and confidence—just what we need. Jesus told this Sister, 'Those who love me much, have great confidence in me. Those who place no limit to their love have great confidence in me without bounds or limit. I cannot disappoint them. You honor me more by the confidence you show me than by all that you could give me. And notice, I respond at once by putting joy into the heart that honors me with confidence.'[8]

The Indwelling of the Holy Trinity – Blessed Elizabeth of the Trinity

The Holy Trinity dwells within each soul that is in the state of Grace. We should talk to the Three Divine Friends who graciously dwell within our souls. They are our Guests. We should be a courteous host. Someone who was such a host was Blessed Elizabeth of the Trinity.

The great teacher of praying to the Holy Trinity within us is Blessed Elizabeth of the Trinity who died in 1906. This French Carmelite Nun taught that we should be attentive to the 'Three' within us and that this requires real recollection. Let me share with you a little about the life of Blessed Elizabeth.

Blessed Elizabeth reached the heights of sanctity, but started out as a strong-willed child. 'You will either be a terror or a saint,' said Mrs. Catez to her daughter Elizabeth. She realized her daughter had a will of iron. The stubborn little girl who demanded her way had inherited the military ways of her ancestors. She was quite a problem until the time of her First Holy Communion when she decided with her iron will to overcome her fault of stubbornness and become a saint.

On the day of her First Holy Communion Elizabeth visited the Carmelite Nuns in her hometown of Dijon, France. The nuns had heard of this iron-willed child, this child who, of late, had determined to become a saint. They had heard that she played the piano brilliantly although her feet could not reach the pedals! During the visit the Mother Prioress explained to Elizabeth that her name signified 'house of God.'

At the age of fourteen Elizabeth decided to become a Carmelite Nun, having heard the word 'Carmel' uttered in her soul one day after Holy Communion. Her mother was determined that Elizabeth would not enter until she was twenty-two. Elizabeth calmly obeyed. The next few years were spent increasing her growth in virtue and being a cheerful companion for her mother.

Prayer was her very existence; starting each day praying before daybreak. Adoration of the Blessed Sacrament, the Holy Rosary and the Way of the Cross were her special prayers. She did penance, even wore a hairshirt and mortified her will. Having asked to suffer the Crown of Thorns, she began to have terrible headaches. She suffered these for two years. They disappeared at the command of her spiritual director. She lived the following motto: 'To have peace one must forget oneself.'

Elizabeth had a cheerful personality. She attended family gatherings and played the piano for the guests. Yet, during these activities, even in the midst of conversation, she remained in prayer. She wrote, 'I cannot be distracted from God.' With her mother, Elizabeth visited Lourdes and was thrilled to receive Holy Communion at the Grotto. She loved the Grotto and said she could not tear herself away.

One day, Father Valee, a Dominican, had a two-hour conversation with Elizabeth. He explained to her that the Blessed Trinity dwelt in her soul. She was immediately inspired to live a life of praise and homage to God dwelling within her. Already, she began to live 'in Heaven' by remaining recollected in the 'Heaven of her soul.' Noise reached only the surface. She desired to lose herself in the Blessed Trinity dwelling within her soul.

At last this 'mystical child' entered the Carmelites. There she was completely at home. As a Carmelite she received the name of Sister Elizabeth of the Trinity. She understood that a Carmelite's life is dedicated to prayer and penance offered for souls. Elizabeth desired to suffer in order to save souls. She wished to offer reparation to God. During her novitiate she passed through the Dark Night of the Soul. She suffered from spiritual dryness and in this Night her virtues were perfected like gold in a furnace. When she made her profession on the Solemnity of Epiphany, 1902, peace again reigned in her soul.

From reading St Paul, Blessed Elizabeth discovered her vocation or mission. She would be a 'Praise of Glory' thus praising God dwelling within her; offering a ceaseless 'Sanctus.' She simply could not understand how a person could carelessly leave God who dwells within the soul to turn to the world and earthly things. 'God dwells within you, do not leave Him so often,' she advised. Even as she worked the sisters noticed her recollected attitude. She once wrote, 'It is wonderful to recall that, except for the vision of seeing God, we possess God as all the Saints in Heaven do. We can surely be with Him always and no one can take us away from Him. He dwells in our souls!'

Blessed Elizabeth's spirituality included love for the Blessed Sacrament and Our Lady, especially devotion to the Mother of Sorrows. She was always pleased when she could spend an entire day in adoration of the Blessed Sacrament in the convent chapel. She once wrote, 'Nothing so reveals the great love of the Sacred Heart as the Holy Eucharist.' She often prayed before the statue of Our Lady of Sorrows and once said. 'I surely love the precious tears shed by the Blessed Virgin Mary.' She taught others to trust in Our Heavenly Mother. She advised a friend that 'there is a Motherly Heart in which you can go and hide: Our Lady's. It has been through every kind of heartbreak, every kind of laceration and through it all remained calm.'

Blessed Elizabeth left a profound teaching about the spiritual life in her letters. Often in them she counselled that one should enter within one's soul and rest in the Presence of the Blessed Trinity. She considered prayer a rest, a relaxation, simply being a child that is safely held and watched over. She advised, 'Be with God who dwells within you and little by little you will become accustomed to this kind of prayer.'

Blessed Elizabeth accepted suffering. She desired to suffer to save souls. She believed that suffering is so special that the Saints in Heaven must 'envy' those still on earth who can suffer to save many souls. She offered her life as a Victim Soul and cheerfully endured her last illness which seems to have been Addison's Disease. She taught others the value of suffering. She wrote, 'There is nothing like the wood of the Cross for kindling in the soul the fire of love.'

Early in 1906 it was noticed that Blessed Elizabeth had become very weak. She made a retreat to prepare for the 'Eternal Retreat.' On August 31, 1906, Sister Elizabeth received an extraordinary grace. The Blessed Trinity was made manifest to her within her soul.

Sick as Blessed Elizabeth was she never omitted prayer. Sitting in a chair by her bed she recited her prayers until one week before she died. One night she was 'tempted' to go back to bed so she immediately knelt down and continued to pray! As Father Philipon, O.P., stated, 'She belonged to the school of saints who seek rest and strength in sacrifice and suffering.'

During the last week of her life, Blessed Elizabeth's stomach was very ulcerated and yet she made frequent and lengthy visits to the Blessed Sacrament. On October 31, she received the last rites. On November 1, she made her confession and received Holy Communion for the last time. On November 9, Blessed Elizabeth of the Trinity died. She desired to lose her sufferings in those of Our Blessed Lord. Her last words were the same as those of St Thérèse of Lisieux; 'Oh, I love Him!' Would she have a mission in Heaven like St Thérèse? Before she died, she proclaimed: 'I believe that in Heaven my mission will be to draw souls to interior recollection by helping them to pray by going out from self to God. I'll teach souls the necessity of a profound inner silence that will allow God to imprint Himself upon souls and transform them into Himself.'

On November 25, the Feast of Christ the King, 1984, the Holy Father beatified Elizabeth Catez, better known and loved as Elizabeth of the Trinity, one of the greatest mystics and spiritual writers of our age.

Theologians have studied the writings of Blessed Elizabeth of the Trinity for many years. Her letters and retreat notes have been studied and commended by a number of theologians, including Father Philipon, O.P. and Father (Cardinal-Elect) Hans Urs Von Balthasar. Blessed Elizabeth's ability to express theology and her talent for writing have been so acclaimed that some have said she 'rivals St Paul' to whom she had a great devotion.

Let us pray to Blessed Elizabeth and read her writings to help us with our conversations with the Holy Trinity dwelling within us.

Contemplatives

Those who give their lives completely to prayer we call contemplatives. These people can be religious such as monks or nuns or they can be lay people who live as contemplatives in the world.

I have met, over the years, many contemplative monks and nuns. One thing I learned very soon was that, although they were dedicated to a life of prayer and to much silence, they were not quiet or shy people. Rather, they were cheerful extroverts, lively and often talkative. Now this might strike some people as strange. Shouldn't contemplatives be shy and naturally quiet? Of course not! The vocation of a contemplative is to talk to God all day long! He or she should be talkative! So, if you're talkative don't let that stop you from becoming a contemplative.

A person can be a contemplative in the world: a contemplative in the marketplace. Most of this person's day is given to prayer. His or her main work is prayer. This was the vocation of Raissa Maritain, the wife of the French Thomistic philosopher, Jacques. She especially dedicated her mornings to prayer. In her journal we read many entries that tell of her times of prayer 'Good prayer in my little room.' Or that she lived 'Silent prayer in the living-room, in spite of the presence of everyone'." She also wrote, 'Ah, how good they are, these mornings given to the Lord!'

Conclusion

I am grateful that you have read my and others' thoughts on conversational prayer. I hope they will inspire you to do conversational prayer. I also hope you will think of you own special ways. For a conversation is something personal. Make it your own. Please believe that although conversational prayer is possible it may be easier for some people. It may come more naturally. If it does not seem to 'flow' give it time. Just like ordinary conversations among people, being a good (or becoming a better) conversationalist takes time and practice. One often reads of the 'practice' of prayer. Yes, prayer is helped by practice.

With prayer, as with many things, a bit of determination helps. And time. As time passes conversational prayer may become 'second nature.' You may find yourself talking to Jesus without almost realising it! It is true that conversational prayer should not be presented as complicated. It is not. I asked a very prayerful lady, whom I know does conversational prayer, how she does it. Her answer was; 'I just talk.' Simple as that. Also, you may do conversational prayer very often, or alternatively find it best to make it only a small part of your prayer life.

However, conversational prayer may just be the 'doorway' for your prayer life for which you have been looking. Many people search for ways to grow in prayer. That is a holy desire. Although as prayer is a matter of the will and of love, not feelings, praying 'better' is something we may never know we are doing. Being more faithful to prayer we can know! And that is what is important. Conversational prayer may help you increase your faithfulness and dedication to praying.

Finally, a request. When you do conversational prayer please be so kind and occasionally mention me. I will be mentioning you, the reader, when I do conversational prayer.

Endnotes

[1] *Crossing the Threshold of Hope* (Knoff 1995).

[2] A very helpful book to inspire you in your conversational prayer is the book *He and I*. It contains the words of Jesus to the French Catholic playwright and actress, Gabrielle Bosis who died in 1950. His words are beautifully conversational. It will inspire you with confidence and trust.

[3] *Discovering How to Pray*. Zondervan, (1990).

[3a] *The Sanctifier*, Luis M. Martinez, available in hardback and softback editions. (ISBN 9780819874122).

[4] For information on this CD try the internet or an online shop.

[5] For information please write to the Carmelite Book Service, Boars Hill. Oxford OX 1 5HB *www.carmelite.org.uk*

[6] *A Game with minutes* is now included in the C. Laubac book *Letters of a modern mystic*. Purposeful Design Publications. Website *www.purposefuldesign.com*.

[7] *Thérèse: Teacher of Prayer*, CTS, 2008.

[8] Tan Books, (1981); Family Publications, Oxford.

Acknowledgements

The Publisher acknowledges the following permissions to quote: Librairie Mediaspoul Paulines, 250 Boul. St Francois Nord, Sherbrooke, Qc. J1E 2B9, Canada for permission to quote much of *He and I* ; Gabrielle Bosis; Institute of Carmelite Studies for the *Holy Trinity* by the Carmelite mystic, Blessed Elizabeth; the Daughters of St Paul for The *Sanctifier* by Archbishop Luis Martinez.

You may contact Brother Craig and learn about his community at *www.monksofadoration.org*.